W9-CFN-218

Adventures & Reflections of an Artist

by
Randall J. Peterson

Edited by
Howard Lestrud & Cliff Buchan

Dedicated to

My wife Kathleen

and our son and daughter
Andrew & Kristine

My artistic ventures would not be
possible without the support of my family.

First Printing: February 2003

ISBN 0-9728273-0-7

Cover Photo:
Morning Sunrise in Bayfield Wisconsin

Cover design and photograph by Randall J. Peterson
Layout and Design by Randall J. Peterson

All artwork and photographs
are created by Randall J. Peterson

Published by

Randall Peterson Designs, Inc.
625 Schilling Circle NW
Forest Lake, MN 55025
651-464-4831

www.lighthouse-artist.com
DotArtist@aol.com

Table of Contents

Acknowledgements

All collectors of my artwork

Woodsedge Gallery and its associates of Forest Lake, MN
Mark "Ace" and Judith Bergerson

ECM Publishers, Inc., All ECM Associates

Howard Lestrud, Cliff Buchan, Michele Kluntz, Howie Burke,
Tina Jensen and Tim Olson

Forest Lake Area Chamber of Commerce

Keeper of the Light and its associates of Bayfield, WI
Apostle Island Cruise Service of Bayfield, WI
Dave Strzok and Mary Grant

Apostle Islands Park Service, Bayfield, WI

Seagull Bay Motel of Bayfield, WI
Mike and Jeanne Goodier

Bayfield, Wisconsin Chamber of Commerce

Lighthouse Digest Magazine
Timothy Harrison and Kathy Finnegan

Jim Merkel of St. Louis, MO

WPBS Television and its Staff in Watertown, NY
Jodi Larsen

Watertown Daily Times of Watertown, NY

Michael Ringer of Alexandria Bay, NY

Northern New York Arts Association
Lynn Newman, The Strejlau Family

Madison County Chamber of Commerce of Winterset, IA

Wyman Wilson of Winterset, IA

Professional Association of Innkeepers International
Jerry Phillips, Executive Director

Select Registry - Susan Moore, Executive Director

Kodiak Coffee and it's associates of Forest Lake, MN
Dick and Anne Tousignant

Elsie Vogel, Teri Ryan, Jim Hermes, Louis Bader,
Bill and Andrea Pedrick

Forward

The history of the world, up until shortly after the invention of the camera, was recorded through artwork, starting from the early caveman's scratches on walls, to the great paintings and of course the many illustrious woodcut engravings that appeared in newspapers in the 1800's, which today are our only view into the past.

Many of our nation's lighthouses, among the oldest standing buildings in the country, and tens of thousands of older buildings have been lost forever, a trend that must not be allowed to continue. A nation that does not save its history is surely a nation that will be lost.

As time marches on with computer generated graphics, fewer and fewer people are training themselves in developing the brain to create works of art created by hand. Randall Peterson has. His ability to create true works of art, through pointillism, to record forever some of our nation's treasured landmarks in a unique art form can only be stated as "outstanding."

One of the benefits of my job is that I get to visit and meet with people from all over the world, many who share the same interest that I do; saving our history for tomorrow's generations. I have often said that preservationists, especially those associated with lighthouses, are all genuinely nice people and one of the nicest of those I have ever met is Randall Peterson; something that you will soon discover for yourself, as you read his story through the pages of this book, that in itself is saving a slice of our history for the future.

Timothy Harrison
President
American Lighthouse Foundation

Introduction

Many people around the world have artwork displayed in their living rooms or dens and some are the original creations of Randall J. Peterson, Forest Lake, who has been an artist for the past 35 years. I was born in Park Falls, Wisconsin, grew up in the Minneapolis/St. Paul area and now reside in Forest Lake, a Minnesota community of 15,000 just north of St. Paul, with my wife Kathleen and daughter Kristine.

I started drawing at the age of nine, working with charcoal and pencil. In the mid 1980s, I did product drawings for Sears Roebuck and Company on a freelance basis. I worked for a graphic arts company from 1977 to 1995 and currently work for a publishing company, ECM Publishers, Inc. Along with my graphics career, I continued my passion for my artwork.

In 1989, I started working with pen and ink as my medium and the style of pointillism. This process or style was first used by French Artist Georges Pierre Seurat in the late 1800s. Most of my originals are 8x10 and each takes about 35 hours to complete. The style of pointillism is created by a series of dots to create the image. I have completed over 100 original drawings.

I've always been fascinated with lighthouses and the stories that surround them -- tales of shipwrecks, rescues, romance and hauntings. Architecturally, I have found that lighthouses are amazingly diverse, each with its own unique design and setting. And, although American lighthouses have been around since the 1700s, many have fallen into disrepair, and are subjected to vandalism and storm damage.

Lighthouses convey a powerful sense of place, some located in stunningly, beautiful remote areas and others anchored securely in the hearts of the communities they serve. My straightforward, black and white style compliments the lighthouse structures, rendering images of simplicity, security and steadfastness. My collection of lighthouse drawings now number 24 with many more to come.

In addition to my lighthouse collection, I've also done a number of commissioned drawings of the most notable and beloved inns found in North America. I have discovered that these lovely structures lend themselves wonderfully to my style of artwork, evoking images that are at once lavish and refined. The nostalgia and romance associated with favorite inns and bed and breakfasts have captivated my imagination, much like my lighthouse artwork. These are places where we can explore the past, get away from the day-to-day, and make our own memories.

Winter Wonderland
Marine on St. Croix

one

In the Beginning

Change, it happens all the time in our world. Some people find it easy to adjust and some people don't. During my career in the graphic arts field, change has happened in many instances, going from traditional layout and design with markers, pencils and pens to the digital process on the computer.

During the transition from conventional design to digital design in the late 1980s, I had an insecure feeling about my occupation in the graphic design field. As a graphic designer, I also had an appetite in the field of fine art. In 1985 I had the opportunity to do pencil drawings of products on a freelance basis, for Sears, Roebuck and Company.

With that insecurity in the back of my mind, I decided to continue my career in graphics and learn as much as I can about the digital process. I also wanted to start drawing as a hobby with the possibility of turning it into a business in the future.

In summer of 1989, I was trying to figure out what I wanted to draw, what would make great subject material. What medium and style do I want to use to create my artwork? After a visit to Como Park Conservatory, a beautiful glass structure housing some of the most exotic flowers and trees from all over the world, I decided to start my collection of drawings. My first drawing is of the Como Park Conservatory in St. Paul. The building, the park grounds with the gardens, the pond reflecting the structure and trees lends itself to a beautiful composition. It brings back wonderful memories of when I was a child and we would go there as a family with friends on Sunday afternoons in the mid 1960s. I now visit Como Park Conservatory with my wife and kids. It's great to go there and have the same feeling I had 40 years ago. It's a place that has withstood change.

As for the style and medium used, I recall a style I enjoyed working in during high school but had no patience to finish a piece of artwork. This style was the fine art of pointillism. I did photo shots of Como Park Conservatory and the grounds to work with a great composition. I started the drawing in the summer of 1989 and completed the work in the fall of that year. It was very challenging to say the least.

I sketched the composition in pencil on illustration board and then started the pointillism process. The results in my mind were very satisfying. The size of the original was 7 inches by 9 inches and took about 24 hours to complete. From my original I created prints and note cards. I had no marketing strategies so I was kind of flying by the seat of my pants.

I contacted the Como Park Conservatory officials to see if they had an interest in selling the prints and note cards in the gift shop. They brought it before their board members and approved the purchase of several prints and note cards. The artwork was also silk screened onto sweatshirts and T-shirts. Sales were brisk.

I felt good about what I accomplished and started thinking of my next composition. After giving it some thought, a theme had come to mind: points of interest in the Minneapolis/St. Paul area. Compositions that people visited as

Como Park Conservatory

children or adults, images that would make great personal gifts as well as corporate gifts.

In the early 1990s I continued with this theme and created various drawings of skylines - St. Paul, Minneapolis, drawings of points of interests in cities surrounding the Twin Cities; Stillwater, White Bear Lake to name a few.

After I completed my St. Paul skyline original in April of 1990, I had prints made and in June of that year, one of the prints was delivered to Minnesota Governor Rudy Perpich's office and given as a gift upon a state visit by President Mikhail and Raisa Gorbachev of the Soviet Union.

St. Paul Mayor James Scheibel ordered framed prints of the St. Paul Skyline and gave them as gifts to dignitaries from other countries when they visited the city of St. Paul.

Meanwhile, I continued to take computer and software classes and adjusted to the digital process. In 1995, I changed jobs from a graphic arts business to a graphics manager at the Forest Lake publication site of ECM Publishers, Inc. There was some adjustment in my position, more tight deadlines and more work with publications from start to finish.

In 1995, I took a year off of drawing to evaluate and see what direction the artwork hobby was taking me. By that time, I completed 27 original drawings. Sixteen of the originals were a part of my collection, 11 were commissioned projects. Up to this point, everything in my collection represented Minnesota subjects and compositions.

After a year and a half of reflecting and a trip to Bayfield Wisconsin, the thought of lighthouses crossed my mind. Lighthouses are common subjects that many people like all over the world. I did some research on lighthouses of Minnesota, then in Wisconsin, and realized there were over 750 lighthouses in the United States and many more all over the world. I learned of there historical significance. The different style structures and the landscapes that surround the lighthouses, made for great subject compositions especially in the style of pointillism. The subject of lighthouses fit into the criteria of my artwork, the history, the memories and continued awareness and preservation of these structures.

I completed two commissioned originals in the summer of 1996. By August of that year, I completed a drawing of the Two Harbors Lighthouse on Minnesotas North Shore of Lake Superior. This was the first in a continuing collection of lighthouse drawings from all over North America.

From 1996 through 2002, I have completed 24 lighthouse compositions. I've done my own photography work and visited all but four of these structures. The four I did not visit I had drawn from photographs supplied by friends. I've been around some of the lighthouses of the Great

St. Paul, Minnesota Skyline

Lakes, the east coast and the St. Lawrence River. My future travels and artwork will include lighthouses and historic structures from Michigan, the southern and western states as well as Canada.

In 1998, I changed positions at ECM Publishers, Inc., I transferred to the Web Printing Plant in Princeton, Minnesota and this is where I continue to be employed as prepress supervisor of three shifts and also work with our commercial accounts in preparing them to send us digital files of their tabloids or newspapers. ECM Publishers, Inc. has been very instrumental with the success of my artwork. There is no conflict of interest with my employment, my artwork and my day to day activities at ECM Publishers, Inc. In fact, it has turned into a partnership with the sheet fed department in the printing of my prints and the printing of this book.

Bridges, castles, victorian houses captured my imagination just like the lighthouses. I added these structures to my collection in the year 2000. These subject matters also fit into my criteria of structures of historic significance.

The objective of my artwork is to draw images that would help rekindle fond memories of these historic structures. These memories include visiting a lighthouse when you were a child, a family picnic at a covered bridge or a stay with a loved one at a Queen Victorian Inn. The objective was also to bring awareness, to help with the preservation of these structures and to educate people of all ages in the fine art of pointillism.

I have been successful in my objectives based on the feedback from teachers, instructors and also in e-mail correspondence from all over the world. I have spoke to many students of various ages and grades about the style of pointillism. It has been a very positive experience for the students and it captured their attention and imagination. As I speak to these classes, the students also get the opportunity to work on an original drawing that I helped create. Below is an example of a letter I receive from one of the teachers.

Stillwater Junior High School
523 West Marsh Street
Stillwater, MN 55082

December 29, 2001

Randall Peterson
625 Schilling Circle NW
Forest Lake, MN 55025-1034

Dear Randy,

It was wonderful to have you speak to the art classes as a guest artist. The students really enjoyed it too. Our school news-broadcast featured your presentation in its section on special lessons in the classroom.

You did a terrific job communicating with the students and showed remarkable endurance conducting five class hours. I cannot emphasize how we appreciated and enjoyed it. I ran into a mother of one of my students in Stillwater and she said her son had talked about it at home. Not only did she note how much he enjoyed it but added that he seldom said much about school, so she knew this was really special.

When school starts on Wednesday we will start working on a pointillism exercise for their graduation standard, a unit they all have to complete for the state requirements. The actual standard is called "group resources" and each student will have a section of a group picture of their class to enlarge in pointillism. Then we will put it all together to recreate a larger version of the photo of their group. It should be fun because the students have had such a good introduction to pointillism and are eager to put this new information to use.

Many thanks for coming to Stillwater Junior High School

7th Grade Art Instructor

Creating and marketing my artwork has been a wonderful experience. To learn about the history of these subjects, listening to the past lighthouse keepers, listening to the volunteers who work at these historic sites is very educational. Creating the artwork has given me the opportunity to visit these structures and to photograph them.

The next few pages are examples of e-mails I've received over the years.

Mr. Peterson, I have a great deal of feeling for the sea and our wonderful lighthouses. I quite enjoy your work as the prints show your care and feelings about the lighthouses. I live in Maine and I have all my life, due to health problems I am not able to leave my home in the cold weather. Therefore I treasure artwork that brings the sea and lighthouses to me. Thank you, please keep up the fine work.

Nance
Wells, Maine

Just wanted to let you know how much I have enjoyed your art works. I am an amateur artist and I am exploring pointillism with inks. I have done a few pieces to date. Thank you for sharing your talents!

Murray
Alberta, Canada

Unbelievable!! Beautiful drawings that really show your talent.

Becky
Ontario, Canada

Hello from Alaska! My great-great-grandfather was the lighthouse keeper for 50 yrs. at Lindesness, Norway. I am starting research for family history. Just wanted to tell you I appreciate your art and desire to preserve lighthouses.

Kathlyne
Kenai, Alaska

Excellent work! I was looking for stippling examples for my son and his art class. (college) He is a kid that just found art having teachers that discouraged it when he was younger. He is in love with it. Just thought I'd give you background on my interest in your work.I did find something else, a real love for your art. It sings with your emotions for it. Good Luck in your endeavors and know that you brought joy to someone who needed it right now.

Brae
Chardon,Ohio

I stumbled upon your web site. I do stippling as well. However, I have been doing it more as a hobby. It was wonderful for me to see your work, one does not see pointillisms very often. I enjoyed your pieces very much.

Leesa
Midland, Michigan

You are a fabulous artist! I love your drawings. I learned to love lighthouses last year when I was blessed to spend some time in New England. You really capture their magic.

Cher
West Point, Utah

I love your drawings of the lighthouses! I am absolutely fascinated with lighthouses! I love the history and I love watching about the haunted lighthouses on TV. There is so much history about them, but a lot of people just think they're an old landmark and nothing more. NOT TRUE!! if I had my way, I would gladly live in a lighthouse for the rest of my life. My kids think I'm obsessed, to a point, I just love the history, it was one of my favorite subjects in school. Thanks

Jacqueline
Houlton, Maine

I am a graphic design student who has just discovered stippling, I think your work is fabulous and inspirational.

Katy
Bellmere, Qld
Australia

I love the way your stippled artwork looks, and we've been learning about the technique in our IB Art and Design Class and so I wrote about your artwork and use of the technique in my art workbook. Just thought I'd let you know I admire your artwork! :o)

Dorene
Palmdale, California

I am just amazed at how much detail is put into your pieces - they look amazing and I look forward to looking at more of your pieces when they are finished.

Alicia
Carrum Downs, Vic
Australia

What beautiful work and such detail! This past year, my girlfriend came up from Delaware, and we went to Boldt Castle for the day. We loved it, and it was one of the best times of our lives. After seeing your sketch, it brought back so many memories for my girlfriend and myself. Thank you once again for bringing a smile to a young couple, very much in love with each other.

Robert
Watertown, New York

I have also received e-mails regarding my artwork from all over the world including South Korea, India, Sweden, The Netherlands, England and the West Indies. Based on the content of many e-mails and letters I have received, I feel I'm accomplishing some objectives of my artwork. Touching the lives of many people through my artwork is very gratifying. Many people say the art of pointillism must be very stressful. For me it is very relaxing, almost a form of meditation. During this time of fast food, fast service, how quick we can get from one place to another, life in the fast lane, for me the art of pointillism has taught me to be patient, a time to slow down and live for today.

While I'm working on compositions, it brings back memories of when I did the photo shoot of a subject. An example of this would be one of my lighthouse compositions, sitting in a boat out on Lake Superior waiting for the fog to lift so I could photograph Sand Island Lighthouse. With the motor turned off and the boat rocking with the waves, once in a while the fog would tease you a bit and you could see a partial outline of the lighthouse. So quiet and peaceful.

When working on a composition for 30 to 50 hours, it gives me time to reflect and appreciate the historic structures past and present.

two

The Style of Pointillism

Pointillism or some artists also refer to it as stippling, was introduced by French artist Georges Seurat in the late 1800s. Seurat perfected this style by using a brush and applying dots of colored paint on a white canvas.

I apply my dots of ink to a white piece of illustration board using a .000 Rapidograph technical pen. I was first introduced to the style of pointillism during my junior year in high school. At that age, I did not have the patience to work with that style. I was able to complete a composition much faster drawing with a pencil.

The style of pointillism is a very delicate process. There is not much room for error. Once the ink is applied, you are committed to the results. Tones and shading are based on the position of the dots applied. Less dots the lighter the area. By adding more dots you are creating a darker or shadowed area.

When I start a new piece of artwork, in most instances, I will visit the location of my composition or subject. I take many photographs of the subject as well as do a few thumbnail sketches for detail purposes and then return to my studio and start drawing. On the next two pages you will see a documented work in progress of the Split Rock Lighthouse original artwork.

Work in Progress – *Split Rock Lighthouse*

This particular drawing took approximately 34 hours to complete. The drawings on this page show the work in progress about every six hours.

I work from my photographs because of the time it takes to create an original. Before I start, I look at the most detailed areas of what I'm going to be drawing. These are the areas I will start with. I will look at the positions of the different tones, the highlights, midtones and shadow areas of the composition.

This will determine where I apply the dots. You must always work light to dark. You can always add dots to make areas darker. Once the dots are on the artwork, you are committed and you can't take them away. You always take into consideration the position of the sun or light source. When working in black and white the importance of tones is extreme. It creates the shape and depth within the composition.

The perspective is also very important in the structures I create. I use the one-point perspective theory. That is where all lines eventually meet at one point to create the depth of a structure. The perspective varies from each original piece of artwork because of the position of the structure. It all depends of the angle captured and plane of which the structure sits, for example, if the structure or object is level in front of you on a hill and you're looking up at it.

After each original is completed, the pen or pens used to create the original are retired. As each original is sold, the pens used to create the original also go to whoever purchases the original.

From an educational perspective, there is great satisfaction and enjoyment in speaking to students of this process. They watch the process with excitement and are eager to try the pointillism process. The one thing I make clear in my visits to classrooms is the difference between digital art and fine art. In this day and age of computers, digital art is

This is a work in progress of the Mayor's Mansion Inn. I start with the most difficult area of the composition.

In this composition, getting the right perspectives and angles is most critical.

Keeping in mind the position of the light source to create your highlights and shadows, this will give the composition shape and depth.

This particular project took over 50 hours to complete. This structure has a lot of detail and character that lends itself to the fine art of pointillism. The Mayor's Mansion Inn is located in Chattanooga, TN

aided by software programs that helps anyone create the same kind of images and artwork effects. In the fine art world it is the raw talent of the individual that has the most impact.

Don't get me wrong, there is a place for digital art in the communication environment. But the purpose again is to make it easier and to provide faster service. The computer and digital world is exciting and changes by the day. But we must not lose our individual talents in the world of fine art.

One question that is quite common is when did I start creating artwork? My earliest recollection would be around the age of five coloring a lot with Crayola colors, just as many other kids did at that age. I do remember lying down on the pews in the St. Paul Cathedral, looking up and noticing the beautiful artwork in the domed ceiling areas of the Cathedral. In hindsight, maybe that's why I have such an interest in old historic architecture.

While I was in elementary school, the Weekly Reader on occasion had an advertisement from a School of Art and Design where they would have kids recreate a simple piece of line artwork and then submit it to have their art skills evaluated. Each month they would have something different to tweak your creative interests. I remember they had a leprechaun one month, followed by a pirate, a fawn, etc. I did these for recreation but did not submit my artwork. This was the starting point of my interest in artwork. Our daughter Kristine has an interest in the arts doing caricature drawings and teaching a dance class.

I had mentioned earlier about taking photographs of my subjects. Over the past many years, I have taken hundreds of photographs. With all the traveling and adventures, it has given me the opportunity to be at the right place at the right time to capture that perfect photo. As I look through the view finder, I try to capture a photo that tells a story.

On one January Saturday morning a few years back, after watching the weather the evening before, the report called for fog along the North Shore of Minnesota. This is a few hours from my home. I decided to drive up there so when the sun would rise, I could capture the beauty of the frost on the trees. I was also planning on taking photos of Split Rock Lighthouse and its winter setting. As I was driving through Duluth, the sunrise just let enough light so I could capture a photo of the fog going under the lift bridge in the Duluth harbor.

As part of my collection I've also photographed a goose napping in front of a covered bridge in Massachusetts, a rainbow over a marina in Bayfield, Wisconsin and a photograph from within the Roseman Covered bridge after a snowstorm. The later is shown below.

three

Lighthouses

After six years of drawing points of interest in Minnesota, I wanted to expand all over North America with my artwork. I needed to draw subjects that all people could relate to, a common subject with historical significance. Whether it was people from coast to coast, or someone from Canada that would also have an interest in a same subject. In 1995, after my first visit to Bayfield, Wisconsin, I realized not only the beauty of the town and its surroundings, Lake Superior, the islands, but also six lighthouses that are on 6 of the 22 islands.

My only other lighthouse experience was with Split Rock Lighthouse on the shores of Lake Superior just north of Two Harbors, Minnesota. After some research on the lighthouses of the United States, I had decided to draw a series of lighthouses. What intrigued me most was how many lighthouses there are in the United States (over 750). Also the history behind many of them is unique and appealing. It's also sad to see how many have deteriorated due to nature and vandals.

When the subject of lighthouses is brought up, the name of Timothy Harrison, publisher of Lighthouse Digest comes to mind. Timothy has a wealth of knowledge and information about lighthouses. His involvement and the time he puts forth with the preservation of lighthouses is unbelievable. Timothy has also authored several books about lighthouses. Between my correspondence with him and reading Lighthouse Digest Magazine, I've learned the importance of the preservation and history of these structures.

Another person who has been very instrumental with my research of lighthouses is Dave Strzok of Bayfield, Wisconsin. Dave is the owner of The Apostle Islands Cruise Service in Bayfield. He has brought many people around the islands and to the lighthouses.

I've had wonderful history lessons and stories told to me from volunteers at the lighthouse locations that I have visited. Listening to authors such as Frederick Stonehouse speak about the hauntings of lighthouses leaves much for the imagination.

In the next several pages, I will be sharing with you many pieces of my lighthouse drawings as well as some of the history, adventures and reflections of my trips to these lighthouses.

Lighthouses of the Great Lakes

Lights of Northern Minnesota...

So the lighthouse series begins. The first lighthouse drawing I completed was the Two Harbors Lighthouse. I did not realize this lighthouse existed until the fall of 1995. After a drive into the town of Two Harbors to see a tugboat in the harbor, we discovered a light shining to the north of where we were standing. Sure enough, it was the Two Harbors Lighthouse. I've driven through Two Harbors on many occasions to visit Split Rock Lighthouse, but never drove to the harbor area. What a great discovery!

Two Harbors Lighthouse

The structure almost takes on the appearance of a school house of the past. The beautiful red brick structure began operating in 1892 and is the oldest operating lighthouse in Minnesota. The tower stands 49 feet tall. The main part of the structure was made into a bed and breakfast.

Split Rock Lighthouse is one of the most photographed lighthouses on the Great Lakes. It is one that I have visited quite frequently. The lighthouse is located just north of Two Harbors, Minnesota on the beautiful shores of Lake Superior. The tower of the lighthouse is 54 feet tall and the cliff it sits on is 130 feet above the lake level.

Split Rock Lighthouse was completed in 1910 along with the keeper's house, the oil house and the fog signal building. One can only imagine the construction process of this lighthouse. Most of the material used had to be brought up the side of the cliff from the lake. The light can be seen 25 miles from shore through its Third Order bi-level lens. Information of various lenses can be found on page 67.

On November 10th of every year, the lighthouse is the site of a ceremony memorializing the ship and crew of the Edmund Fitzgerald. The ship left the port of Duluth with the ship fully loaded with iron ore on a stormy November 10, 1975 heading for Detroit, Michigan. With the storm in full force, the Edmund Fitzgerald sank with its 29 crew members in White Fish Bay, Michigan.

I've attended the ceremony on a couple of occasions and the last one I attended was the 25th anniversary memorial on November 10, 2000. The memorial service was held just outside the lighthouse. Just before the memorial service, the original bell that was recovered from the wreck of the Edmund Fitzgerald was brought to the area of the service. During the service after a few of the readings, the names of the victim's were announced. After each name they rang the original bell one time.

The service ends at dusk around 5:00 p.m. and at that time the lantern of Split Rock Lighthouse is lit. You can see the reflection of the light as it rotates on top of the tower and it is a spectacular sight on the grounds with all the flashing of cameras throughout the park in the crisp cold air of November.

Split Rock Lighthouse

Duluth is the farthest point west of the Great Lakes. Many ships travel through Canal Park, the lift bridge and

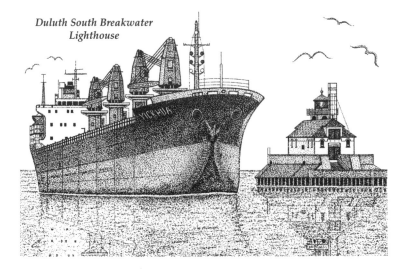

Duluth South Breakwater Lighthouse

the ports of Duluth and Superior, Wisconsin.

The Duluth South Breakwater Outer Lighthouse is one of three lighthouses, located on the breakwaters alongside the channel connecting the inner harbor to Lake Superior in Duluth. It is a great vantage point to see the large ships traveling through the canal. The lighthouse was constructed in 1901.

Lights of the Apostle Islands...

The Apostle Islands are located in northern Wisconsin on Lake Superior 90 miles east of Duluth, Minnesota. There are 22 islands of various shapes and sizes that are a part of the Apostle Islands. Six of the islands have lighthouses on them: Raspberry Island, Outer Island, Devils Island, Sand Island, Michigan Island and Long Island.

Kathy and I discovered the lighthouses of the Apostle Islands during a trip to Bayfield in 1995. We have been to Bayfield at least two or three times a year since then. We travel to Bayfield in July for a get-away trip and the first full weekend after Labor Day as a guest artist at the Keeper of the Light, a nautical store during the annual lighthouse celebration. It is an annual event that has taken place for many years and continues for three weeks in September. It is organized by Dave Strzok and Mary Grant of the Keeper of the Light and the Apostle Islands Cruise Service.

In preparing to create my artwork of the Apostle Island lighthouses, my biggest challenge was to get to all the lighthouses, each one on an island several miles from each other. In 1996, on our summer visit to Bayfield, we took a boat cruise to Raspberry Island and I took many photos of the lighthouse. This particular structure took the shape of a duplex, one side was the keepers quarters and the other

Raspberry Island Lighthouse

side was residence to the assistant keeper.

The grounds and gardens were beautifully maintained and the lighthouse was under some renovating projects to help preserve the structure.

We climbed to the top of the tower and the view was breathtaking, the dark blue color of the waters of Lake Superior was beautiful. In the distance you can see the shores of northern Minnesota. We have visited Raspberry Island on a few other occasions and had a chance to meet "Toots Winfield"(an actor portraying the assistant lighthouse keeper in the 1920s).

I completed the Raspberry Island Lighthouse artwork in 1997. The Raspberry Island Lighthouse was constructed in 1863 and at one time supported the 5th order Fresnel Lens.

The Outer Island Lighthouse was built in 1874 on a red clay bluff 40 feet above Lake Superior. The lighthouse tower stands 90 feet tall and is constructed with white-washed brick. This particular lighthouse was very difficult to photograph and do thumbnail sketches of the Outer Island Lighthouse because of the rough waters. The high waves prevented us from landing on the island. Outer Island as well as Devils Island are the farthest from the mainland.

The Devils Island Lighthouse was completed in 1901 and stands 82 feet tall. What is intriguing about this island are the sea caves that you can see on the shoreline. These sea caves were created from the constant pounding of waves and erosion. The red light flashing through the crystal fresnel lens is visible for 18 miles.

I have been very fortunate to find ways to get out to the islands with the help of new acquaintances and friends from my hometown of Forest Lake, Minnesota. Some of the adventures were associated with trips out to the islands. Some of the photo shoots also included two fishing trips in the late 1990s.

Outer Island Lighthouse

The first fishing trip took us to the lighthouse of Sand Island and Raspberry Island. The group included Cliff, Darrell, Mark, Brian (Hawkeye) and Captain Roger. The fishing was great and the photo shoot was challenging. As we approached Sand Island, you could see a fog bank developing several miles in the distance. My hope is that it was beyond Sand Island. No such luck. As we approached the Island, we were heading right into the fog bank.

Devils Island Lighthouse

The captain said we were about about 50 yards off shore. After 15 minutes, the engines were shut down and we were bobbing up and down with the waves. It was mid-morning and every once in a while the fog would get thin enough where you could make out the outline of the lighthouse.

It was so quiet that morning on Lake Superior you could hear the loons in the distance. My biggest fear was to hear the engines of an approaching ship in the fog. It was actually very relaxing. The fog did finally lift about an hour and a half later and it allowed me to take the photos I needed to capture the detail of the lighthouse.

In years past Kathy and I had visited Sand Island and the lighthouse. The boat docks are at the south end of the island because of the rocks and the shallow depths at the location of the lighthouse on the northeast side of the island. The path from the south side dock to the lighthouse is a two-mile hike across the island.

It is a beautiful groomed partial boardwalk path which leads you through fields of wild flowers and blossoming apple trees. As you come toward the end of the two mile hike, in the opening in front of you is the back side of Sand Island Lighthouse. As you head to the front of the lighthouse the view of Lake Superior is spectacular. In the distance you can see the huge ore boats in the shipping lanes heading for the Twin Ports of Duluth and Superior. The brownstone gothic style lighthouse was built in 1881.

The second fishing and photography trip aboard the Jubilation was more intense with the boat rides to the lighthouses of Devils Island, Michigan Island and Outer Island. The trip included the same group of friends with the addition of Darrell's son Andy and my son Andrew.

This trip was special because I also had time to spend with my son. He lives for fishing and hunting. It was great bonding with him in his environment of fishing. Sometimes I'd get so wrapped up in my artwork, something like this is needed to remind me I have a family and other

Sand Island Lighthouse

responsibilities.

On this trip we spent three days out in Lake Superior and camped on two of the islands. The first day we headed for Devils Island. This Island is one of the farthest points from the City of Bayfield. I took over three hours to get to the island. It was a beautiful sunny morning and the white steel lighthouse structure was well defined with the bright blue skies in the background.

Around 11:00 a.m. that same day, we fished for about an hour and then headed for Rocky Island. This is the island we were camping on the first night. As we approached the island dock at 1:00 p.m. we could see the park ranger walking to the dock.

As we docked, the park ranger introduced herself as Ranger Julie and was there to greet and welcome us to the island. After she checked the camping permits she said she had some ginger snap cookies baking in the oven at the rangers cabin and she would bring some down in a few minutes.

We had asked her if she had her lunch and she said no. We invited her to have lunch with us as long as she is bringing the cookies. With the eight guys in our group and Ranger Julie, we had a light lunch of sandwiches, veggies and chips and of course the delicious and still warm, Ranger Julie's ginger snap cookies.

After lunch Captain Roger lit one of his cigars. Ranger Julie filled us in on the facts of Rocky Island and information on Stockton Island, the island we were going to be camping on the next evening. Captain Roger has a great sense of humor, loves to laugh, talk and tell stories about his boating experiences. He also has a great sense of where the fish were.

As Captain Roger finished smoking his cigar, he was getting ready to extinguish it in the lake when Ranger Julie called out, "Captain, if that butt goes in the lake, yours does too!" Ranger Julie then went over the hiking trails of the island and we then set up camp.

The second day we started out fishing and we were not having much

Michigan Island Lighthouses

luck, so we headed out to Outer Island. With the rough waters, we were there for a short time, just long enough to get a few photographs.

The Long Island Lighthouse

We then made our way to Stockton Island, docked and unloaded our camping gear. Some of us regained our appetites after losing our breakfast in the high waves around Outer Island to enjoy a light lunch. After lunch we did go fishing just a short distance from Stockton Island. We had much better luck and caught salmon and lake trout.

Later that afternoon, we traveled to Michigan Island to photograph its two lighthouses. The grounds of the lighthouses were gorgeous with its manicured gardens. This island is very unique because of its history. The small rough stone lighthouse was constructed in 1857. This lighthouse was constructed on the wrong island. It was supposed to be built on Long Island. Fifty years later, a 112 foot cylinder steel tower was brought in to the island from its original location at Schooner's Ledge on the Delaware River near Philadelphia.

Long Island also has two lighthouses (shown in the artwork on the previous page), the lighthouse (in the lower left) is the Chequamegon Point Light and the other is known as the La Pointe Light. Both lighthouses were constructed in 1895.

My adventures on the Apostle Islands could not have been possible without the help of my friends and new acquaintances. My fishing friends from Forest Lake, the businesses of Bayfield, The Bayfield Chamber of Commerce, Mary Grant from The Keeper of the Light store and Dave Strzok from the Apostle Islands Cruise Service who provided me with a lot of history of the Islands as well as the Park Service of the Apostle Islands National Lakeshore.

Other Lights on the Great Lakes ...

In my research of lighthouses, I have not found two lighthouses that look the same. They are all unique in their own way. There are short lighthouses, tall lighthouses, lighthouses that look like a house. Lighthouse towers are round, others are square and some even take an octagon shape.

Buffalo Main Lighthouse

Many different materials are used to construct lighthouses. Some of the structures are built out of stone, wood, bricks, steel, and concrete. The height of the lighthouses must have been based on the terrain and height of the land it sits on.

Kathy and I flew to Buffalo, New York in 1997 for my photo shoot and thumbnail sketches of lighthouses on Lake Erie and Lake Ontario. We also took a few days of vacation and traveled to Niagara Falls. After a few days in Niagara Falls, we drove from the shores of Lake Erie in Barcelona, New York to the farthest point east of the Great Lakes, Cape Vincent, New York. The landscape was similar to that of Northern Minnesota.

Our travels brought us to the Buffalo Main Lighthouse. The Buffalo Main Lighthouse known as the "Chinaman's Light," is located in Buffalo, New York on the Coast Guard Base at the juncture of the Buffalo River and Lake Erie. The structure stands 68 feet tall, the octagon tower was constructed with a buff colored Queenston limestone. The small structure next to the lighthouse is Buffalo's famous bottle light. The area in which you can view the lighthouse is an area of beautiful gardens and walking paths.

Many of the lighthouses have gift stores or museums of historical information. At many of the sites are volunteers who give their time and energy being part of the history. Whether it's working in the gift shops, the museums, the grounds and gardens or maintenance of the buildings, you can see in their eyes they love what they do and it's from the heart. This was quite evident in many of the lighthouses, bridges and historic structure we have visited.

The Barcelona Lighthouse, located in Barcelona, New York on Lake Erie, 20 miles southwest of the Dunkirk

Lighthouse, is not included in my collection at this time. Because of its historic significance, I would mention it in this book. The construction of this lighthouse was completed in 1829, making it one of the oldest lighthouse structures on the Great Lakes. The Barcelona Lighthouse stands 40 feet tall and was constructed from rough split stone. It was the first public building in the United States to be illuminated by natural gas.

Our travels then brought us to the Dunkirk Lighthouse. The Dunkirk Lighthouse is located in Point Gratiot, New York on the shores of Lake Erie near the City of Dunkirk, New York. It was constructed in 1876 and the lighthouse tower stands 62 feet tall. A covered passage connects the light tower to the two-story, eight-room stick style keepers dwelling.

Dunkirk Lighthouse

What was challenging about the Dunkirk Lighthouse is the keepers quarters, the house which had many different angles in the roof line. The most difficult part of this artwork was to make sure perspective was correct. This was a busy piece with all the detail in the trim. We spent many hours at this lighthouse that is rich in history. The volunteers were very friendly and gave us a personal tour of the structure.

The Fort Niagara Lighthouse is located in Youngstown, New York, at the juncture of the Niagara River and Lake Ontario. This stone structure went into service in 1872. The The octagon lighthouse stood 50 feet tall until the year 1900 when they extended the light another 11 feet. The light is visible 25 miles out into Lake Ontario.

The lighthouse is located within Fort Niagara State Park From the grounds in the distance on a clear day, a person can see the skyline of Toronto, Canada.

Other lighthouses we visited along the way included the Sodus Point Lighthouse located in Sodus Point, New York. This lighthouse was a limestone structure constructed in 1871. The 45 foot square tower also was attached to a 2 1/2 story dwelling. The Oswego West Pierhead Light in Oswego, New York and the Selkirk Lighthouse in Selkirk, New York were others we visited.

Most of the lighthouses that we have visited since 1995, have access to the lantern room on top of the lighthouses. The lighthouses that did not have access were either closed for the season or under renovation. The ones that were open, we climbed to the top and the views were breathtaking.

The Charlotte-Genesee Lighthouse sits on the banks of the western banks of the Genesee River where it empties

Fort Niagara Lighthouse

into Lake Ontario near the City of Rochester, New York. The limestone tower was constructed in 1822 with the addition of the brick residence in 1863. This lighthouse was saved from possible demolition in 1965 with the help of the petitions of students from Charlotte High School.

Charlotte-Genesee Lighthouse

The Tibbetts Point Lighthouse is located at the entrance of the St. Lawrence River on Lake Ontario in Cape Vincent. New York The 69 foot white round stucco lighthouse was constructed in 1854. At this time, the Tibbetts Point Lighthouse is the only one in my lighthouse collection that has the light on. Some of the most beautiful sunsets take place on the grounds of Tibbetts Point.

Tibbetts Point Lighthouse

Thirty Mile Point Lighthouse was constructed in 1875 at the mouth of Golden Hill Creek on Lake Ontario. The lighthouse is located in the town of

Thirty Mile Point Lighthouse

Barker, New York, 30 miles east of the Niagara River. The lighthouse stands over 60 feet tall and was constructed with hand carved limestone. It also sits on the grounds of Golden Hill state park.

The Chicago Harbor Lighthouse was constructed in 1893 at the mouth of the Chicago River. The light supported a third order Fresnel lens. It was moved to its current location in the harbor at the end of Navy Pier in 1919 near the shores of Lake Michigan. In the background of this lighthouse is the Chicago skyline.

Future travels in the Great Lakes Region will take me to the state of Michigan to capture some of the beauty of the lighthouses on Lake Michigan and Lake Huron. Michigan has 114 lighthouses. Of my travels some of the lighthouses of Michigan will become part of my collection.

Chicago Harbor Lighthouse

Coastal Lighthouses

February 2000 brought me to the New England States. Prior to my pilgrimage out east, much research was needed to decide what lighthouses to see and how to find them. The trip was going rather short (four days) and many miles. With the amount of miles I was going to be driving, Kathy did not want me to travel alone. Dan Haasl, a friend of mine from Forest Lake, who also has a great interest in lighthouses accompanied me on this trip.

There was much research needed, planning our route, selecting the lighthouses we were going to photograph and where to find them. The research to finding them was very important. Because of people trespassing and vandalism that takes place, some of the lighthouses are not advertised where they are located and are difficult to find. People who have a love for lighthouses have no problem in finding them. Some lighthouses are located on private property and people must respect their privacy.

On the first day, Dan and I flew to Boston, Massachuettes, after picking up the rental car, we drove to Newport, Rhode Island. Photographed the Newport and Castle Hill lighthouses. From the Newport Light, in a distance I could see the Rose Island Lighthouse. From the Castle Hill Lighthouse, in the distance I could see the Beavertail Lighthouse.

We then drove to Watch Hill, Rhode Island, the location of the Watch Hill Lighthouse. I had been to this lighthouse in the summer of 1988 during the height of the tourist season. After the photo shoot of Watch Hill, we ended the first day in Mystic, Connecticut.

The second day brought us to the Mystic Seaport, a very

picturesque area of Connecticut. This was my third trip to this area. After visiting the lighthouse at Mystic Seaport, we drove to New London, Connecticut to see the New London Lighthouse. From the beaches of New London, You could see the New London Ledge Lighthouse. This was the farthest point west and south of our trip. We then headed east to Stonington, Connecticut to see the Stonington Lighthouse. Our journey then took us up to Wells, Maine, home of Lighthouse Depot.

We visited Lighthouse Depot and met Kathleen Finnegan, Assistant Editor and Advertising Manager of Lighthouse Digest Magazine. Kathleen gave as a tour of the store as well as the museum of historical lighthouse items. Then she introduced us to Timothy Harrison, Publisher and Editor of Lighthouse Digest Magazine. Timothy is very instrumental in the preservation of lighthouses. Through his associations of various organizations he has helped save several lighthouses. We had a chance talk to Timothy about some of the lighthouses of Maine before we continued our journey that afternoon.

My wife and I also met with Timothy and Kathleen in Bayfield, Wisconsin at the Annual Lighthouse Celebration in September 2001. They were planning to fly in from Maine, but because of the terrible September 11, 2001 terrorist attack, their flight had been cancelled. They had a scheduled speaking engagement at the Lighthouse Celebration in Bayfield the Saturday after the attack. Timothy and Kathleen thought about it and decided they would still keep the speaking engagement and drive to Bayfield from Wells, Maine. It was a very inspiring speech about the awareness and preservation of lighthouses all over North America.

Dan and I continued our trip on that second day and it was about 3:00 p.m. We drove to Cape Neddick, Maine, home the Cape Neddick Lighthouse also referred to as the "Nubble Lighthouse." We headed north to Portland, Maine and found our way to Portland Head Lighthouse. We ended our day in Augusta, Maine.

On the third day, our plan was to drive to Lubec, Maine and do an early morning photo shoot of the West Quoddy Lighthouse. To do this we had to leave Augusta by 3:00 a.m. This lighthouse is located on the most eastern point of the United States. The early morning drive was well worth it with the spectacular sunrise at the lighthouse. At this point we were the farthest north and east of our trip. We were now heading back toward Boston, but along the way we visited many more lighthouses on the coast of Maine. Maine has 68 lighthouse on its beautiful, rugged coast.

After photographing and enjoying the beauty around the West Quoddy Lighthouse, we stopped at the Prospect Harbor Lighthouse located in Prospect Harbor, Maine. Due to time constraints we drove for a few hours along the coast to the town of Rockland, Maine. From downtown Rockland in the harbor, you can see Rockland Breakwater Light.

We ended our third day in Rockland by going to the Owls Head Lighthouse and the Marshall Point Light in Port Clyde Harbor. Both lights are located near Rockland.

On the Fourth and final day of the trip we left Rockland in the fog. With our flight not leaving until 5:00 p.m. We visited a few more lighthouses before we returned to Boston. We stopped at the Portsmouth Harbor Lighthouse on the grounds in Fort Constitution near New Castle, New Hampshire. Our final lighthouse visit was to the

Annisquam Lighthouse in Ispwich Bay near the City of Lanesville, Massachusetts. Then we were off to Boston to catch our flight back to Minneapolis.

In four days, we traveled 1300 miles and saw 21 beautiful lighthouses. Usually when I take trips I try to spend as much time on site as possible, but because I'm employed full time, vacation time also becomes an issue of how I want to spread them out. Many thanks to my friend Dan Haasl of Forest Lake. With his help in navigating us to many of the lighthouse and his turn driving, this trip would not have been possible.

The next three pieces of artwork on the next few pages are the results of this trip, the lights of Cape Neddick, Portland Head and Mystic Seaport.

The Cape Neddick Lighthouse is also known as the Nubble Light. The lighthouse was completed in 1879 and is located on a rocky island referred to as the nubble in Cape Neddick near York, Maine. The cast-iron tower stands 41 feet tall and supported the fourth-order lens. During the Christmas holiday season, the lighthouse and buildings are decorated with many lights. The lights luminate and reflect in the water which makes for a beautiful, picturesque scene.

The Portland Head Lighthouse, one of the most famous lighthouses you see in books, magazines, calenders is one of the most photogenic lighthouses in America. The lighthouse is located in Cape Elizabeth, Maine. When I was at this lighthouse doing my photographs, the setting was spectacular. Construction of the lighthouse began in the year 1790 with the tower rising to the height of 72 feet. The lighthouse in the distance is the Ram Island Ledge Light.

Cape Neddick (Nubble) Lighthouse

When I did the photo shoot of Portland Head Lighthouse, it was the perfect setting. It was about 4:15 p.m. on a cold, late February afternoon with a little mist in the air. As I was walking and snapping photos, on the grounds of the lighthouse you see and hear the waves over and over crashing on the large rocks below me, you could feel the energy. The light was rotating on top of the tower. The weather conditions demonstrated why they build lighthouses.

After I was finished taking my photos, I continued to walk the grounds looking at the structures and the landscape surrounding the structures. As I walked up to the light tower, I put my hand on the lighthouse and thought to myself, how wonderful to have a structure withstand the force of mother nature after all these years. To see a lighthouse that was commissioned by George Washington still standing and the engineering of this structure back in the late 1700s is truly amazing.

The Mystic Seaport Lighthouse is located in Mystic, Connecticut home of "Mystic Pizza." The lighthouse is of a replica in design to the Brant Point on Nantucket Island in Massachusetts. The lighthouse stands 26 feet tall and is nestled amongst the ships in Mystic Seaport, an authentically restored 19th century coastal village.

The town of Mystic and the surrounding area leaves great opportunities for photographers and artists alike. The lighthouse is supported by a fourth order Fresnel lens.

On the shores of the outer banks of North Carolina, you will find America's tallest lighthouse, Cape Hatteras Lighthouse. The lighthouse is located near the city of Buxton, North Carolina and was built in 1869. The lighthouse

Portland Head Lighthouse

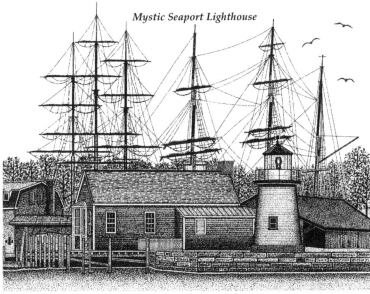

Mystic Seaport Lighthouse

stands 280 feet tall and the signal is visible for 20 miles. 268 stairs lead to the top of the lighthouse.

During the American Civil War, the original lighthouse was attacked by both Union and Confederate forces. Over the years, three different Cape Hatteras Lighthouses have existed.

In the early 1990s, it was quite evident from year to year the erosion that was taking place, something had to be done to save this lighthouse. Much research was done with some options available. The best long term solution was to move the lighthouse away from the shore. It was felt that if the lighthouse was not moved, it could topple over during a high category hurricane. After the decision and the funding approved to move Cape Hatteras Lighthouse, the work began in the spring of 1999.

On June 17, 1999 with the engineering completed, the beams, the tracks and the hydraulic jacks in place, the clearing of the corridor complete, it was time for the historic lighthouse to start the trip to its new home. At 3:05 pm that afternoon, it was recorded the first movement of the lighthouse 4 inches away from its original foundation marking the start of it's 2,900-foot journey.

During the next three weeks the lighthouse moved various distances each day. On July 9, 1999 Cape Hatteras Lighthouse reached the final destination over the top of the new foundation at 1:23 pm. The move was expected to take four to six weeks to complete, but it was accomplished in 23 days. After a few months, the project was complete and Cape Hatteras withstood two hurricanes, Dennis and Floyd. The relighting ceremony took place in mid November 1999 and it opened back up to the public in May of 2001.

Cape Hatteras Lighthouse

The coverage of the move was wonderful. I could track it on a daily bases via the Internet and the coverage was also covered well by the writers of Lighthouse Digest Magazine during the year of 1999. A part of American history was preserved thanks to many people and organizations.

Cape Lookout Lighthouse is located on the south end of the Core

Cape Lookout Lighthouse

Banks and is part of the Cape Lookout National Seashore. The lighthouse is located near the city of Beaufort, North Carolina and construction was completed in 1859. The diamond pattern design was added in 1873 to make it a better daymark. The lighthouse stands 161 feet tall.

Amelia Island Lighthouse is located by Fernandina Beach, Florida. The lighthouse was completed in 1838. It sits 170 feet above sea level with a beam that's visible for 19 miles at sea. The light-

Amelia Island Lighthouse

Lime Kiln Lighthouse

house tower stands just over 60 feet tall.

Lime Kiln Lighthouse is located on the west side of San Juan Island (Washington State) in Lime Kiln State Park facing Haro Strait. The lighthouse was built in 1919.

Other Lighthouses

The Sunken Rock Lighthouse is located on Bush Island on the St. Lawrence River near the town of Alexandria Bay, New York. The lighthouse was constructed in 1847. In the background is Boldt Castle which is located on Heart Island, The St. Lawrence River connects the Atlantic Ocean with Lake Ontario. The depth in this part of the river is 250 feet.

Sunken Rock Island Lighthouse

My travels will some day take me to the lighthouses of the Pacific coast as well as the Southern states and the coasts of Canada. Some of the lighthouses along the way will become part of my collection of artwork. Unfortunately, I can only do so many originals to add to my collection as well as commissions per year.

Lighthouses convey a powerful sense of place, some located in stunningly, beautiful remote areas and others anchored securely in the hearts of the communities they serve. Let's help keep their historical significance through awareness and preservation.

Lighthouse Lens

In this chapter, names of lens were mentioned in association with some of the lighthouses. The most common being the Fresnel Lens. Prior to 1850, the light source was the whale-oil lamp. During the 1850s, the Fresnel Lens replaced whale-oil lamps. The Fresnel Lens was invented in France by physicist Augustin Fresnel in 1822.

The Fresnel lens is built with an array of glass prisms and a bull's-eye lens mounted in a brass framework. The lens had six sizes called orders. The sixth order Fresnel lens was the weakest, was used in lighthouses in lakes and harbors. The first order Fresnel lens was the strongest and used more on the coastal lighthouses.

Each lighthouse has its own light characteristic to determine its identity. The periods of flashes distinguish the identity of the lighthouses.

four

Bridges

When one mentions covered bridges, the first thing that comes to mind are The Bridges of Madison County, or the beautiful images of the covered bridges in the New England states with the fall colors and the the scenic hills in the background.

There are many covered bridges as well as historic uncovered bridges all over the United States. I have visited specific bridges in Minnesota, Wisconsin, Iowa and in the New England states. A trip to Winterset, Iowa, brought me to the bridges of Madison County. At one time, there were 19 covered bridges in this county, today five remain standing with a sixth one that was just destroyed by fire believed to be started by an arsonist.

I decided to add bridges to my collection of renderings because of their historical significance and carries the same theme and values of my lighthouse collection. The bridges have many childhood memories for many and the structures and landscapes lend themselves well to my style of artwork.

Why were the covered bridges covered? My thought was that they served an area of protection for people and horses as they crossed the rivers and creeks. After visiting with Wyman, a next door neighbor to the Roseman Covered Bridge, I learned a lot about the history of covered bridges. The main reason the bridges were covered was to protect and preserve the base of the covered bridges. The roof and sides were easier to maintain and replace, but the base with the timbers and engineering that was involved would make it time consuming and costly to replace.

The covered bridges of Madison County...

All but one of the covered bridges are within miles of Winterset. The Imes Covered Bridge is located in the City of St. Charles, IA. On September 3, 2002, while I was writing this book, The Cedar Covered Bridge was destroyed by fire. All indications are this fire was intentionally set.

The Cedar Covered Bridge was built in 1883 by Benton Jones. It was the only bridge open to vehicles and the

This was a photo of the Cedar Bridge was taken by Randall J. Peterson on Feb. 2, 2002 with the branches graced with the highlights of a fresh snow cover.

length of the bridge was 76 feet. It was featured on the cover and in the novel by Robert James Waller "*The Bridges of Madison County.*" In 1993 the bridge was the setting for a broadcast of the Oprah Winfrey show.

I've seen this bridge in the summer with all its flowers on both sides and the trees in full bloom. In the winter we see a high contrast of dark branches and bright snow. In October of 2002, I visited the burned bridge and I could feel the hurt put on this community.

It is a devastating sight and raises the question, how could a person do this. When they do apprehend this cold hearted soul or souls that set this fire, they should be charged with "a death of a bridge." It is devastating to lose a bridge to the elements of mother nature, but when it's the case of arson, it is horrifying.

This was a photo of the Cedar Bridge was taken by Randall J. Peterson on Oct. 2, 2002 after the work of an arsonist on Sept. 3, 2002

When I was at the Cedar Bridge, a gentleman was standing at the one end of the bridge just staring at its charred ruins. After a bit, I asked him if he was from the area. He told me that he grew up about a quarter mile from the bridge. He said that he and his sister played on the bridge every morning before the bus would bring them to their elementary school. I happened to have some of the Cedar Bridge photos I took last February in the trunk of my car and had gave him one. He was very grateful as he left the site, for his home a quarter mile away. The communities of Madison County may have the bridge rebuilt at the cost of $1 million.

The Roseman Covered Bridge is featured in the novel *"The Bridges of Madison County"* written by Robert James Waller in 1992 and also a movie version directed by Clint

The Roseman Covered Bridge

Eastwood in 1995 starring Eastwood and Meryl Streep. The bridge was constructed in 1883 by Benton Jones. The length of the bridge is 107 feet. It was renovated in 1992. With the beautiful setting of this covered bridge, many weddings have taken place at this bridge.

The Holliwell Covered Bridge was completed in 1880 and built by Benton Jones. It stretches across the Middle River just outside the city limits of Winterset. It is the longest of the bridges at the length of 122 feet. The Holliwell Covered Bridge was renovated in 1995 and was featured in the movie "*The Bridges of Madison County.*"

The Hogback Covered Bridge is located at its original location three miles north of Winterset. It was built by Benton Jones in 1884 and the length of the bridge is 97 feet. The beauty of the rolling hills and the winding road that leads you to the bridge is magnificent.

The Cutler-Donahoe Covered Bridge was moved to its present location in Winterset's City Park in 1970. The bridge was built in 1880 by Eli Cox. The length of the bridge is 79 feet and the only one of the six that featured a pitched roof.

The Imes Covered Bridge was moved to City of St. Charles, IA in 1977. It was originally located over the middle River near Patterson, IA. The bridge was constructed in 1870 and is the oldest of the remaining bridges. The length of the bridge is 81 feet.

Other bridges...

In 1991 Kathy and I were visiting some friends in Meriden, Connecticut and had the opportunity to see our first covered bridge, the Old Comstock Covered Bridge located on the southeast side of East Hampton, Connecticut on the Salmon River. As we approached the covered bridge, we saw several adults with their children fishing from the banks of the river as well as some in the river with wadders on. With families enjoying picnic lunches, it was a very picturesque sight.

The Old Comstock Covered Bridge was built in 1873 using the Howe truss design. The overall length of the bridge is 110 feet, the covered portion 80 feet and the open portion 30 feet. The bridge was listed on the National Register of Historic Places in 1976.

With my research on various bridges, I knew that there are hundreds of covered bridges in the United States and Canada. If you visit these bridges during the summer months, you notice all the colors of the landscapes which makes it picturesque. If you visit the same bridges during

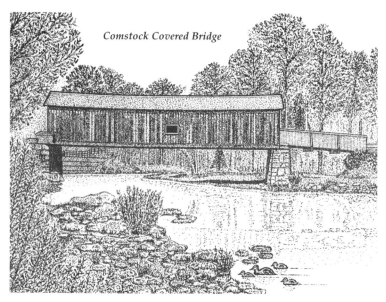

Comstock Covered Bridge

the winter months, it completely sets a different mood, more peaceful and serene. One of the reasons so many covered bridges were built in the late 1880s was because of the abundance of trees in the United States.

The Stillwater Bridge sits on the St. Croix River transporting vehicles and people between Minnesota and Wisconsin. The bridge was built in 1931 and the spans a distance of 1,050 feet. On the Minnesota side the entrance of the steel and iron bridge is the City of Stillwater.

Many events and festivals take place in the parks located near the bridge. Stillwater is

Entrance to the Stillwater Bridge

Stillwater Bridge

the birthplace of Minnesota. The historic lift bridge is in the National Register of Historic places.

I have drawn many uncovered bridges in different communities. There are so many styles and designs of bridges across North America all unique in there own way. Below, is a bridge crossing the West Branch of the Rum River in Princeton, Minnesota. This piece of artwork was part of a fund-raiser for ECM Publishers, Inc. with proceeds going to community needs.

The historic Stone Arch Bridge, in Minneapolis, Minnesota was completed in 1883. It was built by railroad magnate James J. Hill. The length of the slightly curved stone railroad bridge was 2,100 feet and had 23 stone arches. The bridge crosses the mighty Mississippi River connecting the St. Anthony area to downtown Minneapolis. Today it is open to pedestrians and trolleys.

The Stone Arch Bridge, also known as the James Hill

Princeton Bridge

Bridge, featuring the two cardinal birds in front of the bridge was a drawing created in 1994. It was one of two pieces of artwork that the originals were black and white, and the limited edition prints had a splash of color behind the birds. The other piece of artwork with color added in the limited edition prints was titled "Visions," with the subject of two blue jays looking toward the Split Rock Lighthouse.

Both originals were donated for fund-raisers, the James Hill Bridge original to help raise funds for a community gazebo and the "Visions" original to the Lions Clubs International to raise funds for the LCIF Sightfirst program.

I look forward to my future travels and adventures to other bridges across North America and to learn the history of them. My goal is to bring continued awareness and preservation through my artistic ability.

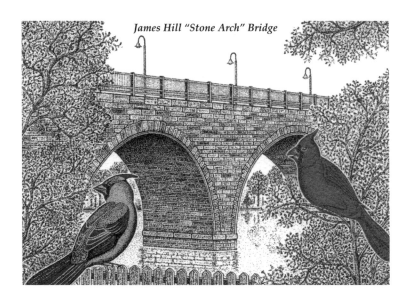
James Hill "Stone Arch" Bridge

five

Historic Structures

When historic structures come to mind, I think about castles, inns, bed and breakfast establishments, court houses, capitol buildings and many towns and cities that have historic districts within them. The historic structures also fell under the criteria of what I wanted to accomplish through my artwork. The memories, preservation and awareness of these structures. Also, with the magnificent detail and design applied themselves wonderfully with my style of artwork

I have done historic structures such as a capitol building bed and breakfast inns and knew someday I would be doing castles. As fate had it, I did my first castle sooner than expected.

In July 2001, I received a letter from WPBS-TV in Watertown, New York. The letter asked for a donation of a piece of artwork to be included in the WPBS-TV annual art auction. After reading the letter, my first thought was I do donate plenty to organizations around Minnesota, why would I want to donate to a fund-raising event in Watertown, New York. I decided to think about it and I set the letter aside.

Two weeks later, in mid-August, I received an e-mail from Jodi Larsen of WPBS-TV. I remembered the letter from them in July, and it raised my curiosity of all the interest of my artwork in Watertown, New York. The e-mail letter asked if I would be interested in being a featured artist at their annual art auction in November 2001 at WPBS-TV in Watertown, New York. Jodi Larsen is the events coordinator with the station.

My curiosity and interest finally made me call Jodi Larsen. Jodi had told me the history and success of the annual fall art auction they've done for 20 years. WPBS-TV is a non-profit public television station, serving Northern New York and Southeastern Ontario, Canada. The station serves approximately 2.2 million viewers.

Every year WPBS-TV features two artists and highlight their works of art throughout the four-day auction. The station also encourages and invites artists from Ontario and Northern New York to donate artwork and be a part of the auction. The criteria after being selected as a featured artist was to donate some original artwork as well as limited edition prints in exchange for the station to do a 30-minute documentary of the featured artist and have them at the station for the four days.

WPBS-TV also promoted the auction and the featured artists, running the 30 minute documentary of each featured artist days prior to the auction. They also advertise and promote the event through newspaper ads and other television stations.

To introduce my artwork to that part of the country as well as the style of pointillism was a wonderful opportunity and I felt quite honored that WPBS-TV wanted me as one of its featured artists with all the artistic talent in that part of the country. I accepted the invitation.

During the first week of September 2001, I called Jodi to set up the arrangements to have the documentary produced and had it scheduled to be shot and produced in Northern Minnesota on the beautiful shores of Lake Superior at the site of Split Rock Lighthouse. While I had Jodi on the phone, I was curious why choose me as a featured artist and wondered how she found out about me and my artwork.

Jodi said she had taken the position of events coordinator in the spring of 2001. As she was putting the art auction together, she was identifying and selecting the 2001 featured artists for the event. One day Jodi was cleaning and reorganizing the desk of her predecessor.

As she was going through the file folders, she had saw a magazine article cut out of the November 1999 issue of Lighthouse Digest Magazine. It was a feature article "Randall Peterson: Spotlighting Lighthouses With Little Dots" by writer Jim Merkel, an article about me and my style of artwork.

The article listed my e-mail and that is how Jodi contacted me. She thought my artwork was unique and something that the art auction did not have in the past. The other featured artist was wildlife artist Andrew Hoag of Bethany, Ontario. Andrew's works of art are very realistic and have much detail. It was a great experience to meet an artist like Andrew, understanding his ideas and perspectives in what goes into his original artwork

With the documentary to be shot in Minnesota the third week in September. WPBS-TV scheduled two travel days and a day and a half of shooting at Split Rock Lighthouse. Just as the airline tickets were to be ordered, the unthinkable happened with the terrorist attacks of September 11, 2001. During that week it was almost surrealistic, like it was a dream, listening to many tragic stories that changed the lives of thousands and thousands of people.

With the airlines still sorting out schedules and the new security measures in place at the airports, it made it impossible due to time constraints to get WPBS-TV to Minnesota to do the documentary. Kathy and I decided to take a week and drive to Watertown, New York. It was a wonderful drive with some of the trees still showing off their fall colors in Wisconsin, Illinois, Indiana, Ohio, Pennsylvania and New York.

The timing was great because of our busy schedules, it was wonderful to have the time together. It was our longest road trip in 13 years. It was three weeks after the attacks of 9/11/01 and I'm sure like many other people, it brought life in prospective and families closer together.

Jodi Larsen made arrangements for parts of the documentary to be shot on Heart Island, home to Boldt Castle on the St. Lawrence River near Alexandria Bay, New York. Boldt Castle has a very unique story behind it. The castle has the same design as castles of the 16th century of northern Europe. The structure stands six stories tall and has over 120 rooms.

The castle was under construction in the early 1900s by George Boldt and was being built for his wife Louise. In 1904, with the castle almost complete, George Boldt who was on Heart Island, received an unexpected letter notifying him of the passing of his wife. He was so heartbroken that he sent the 300 construction workers home and left the island of which he never returned.

Over the years, Boldt Castle fell to vandals, Mother Nature and materials removed for use during war times. The Boldt Estate was sold to the Noble family and eventually purchased by Thousand Islands Bridge Authority for

$1.00 in 1977 with the understanding that it could be opened up to the public for tours and not used for commercial enterprises. The proceeds from the admission charge of touring the Castle go towards the restorations of the property. The other part of the documentary was shot at Tibbetts Point Lighthouse in Cape Vincent, New York.

After Kathy and I returned to Minnesota, I decided one of the originals I wanted to donate was a pen and ink drawing of Boldt Castle. When we first saw the castle, its charm, character and dimension captured my imagination immediately. It was to be a tremendous challenge and indeed it was. It took a four- week period (76 hours) to complete the original of Boldt Castle.

After those four weeks passed, Kathy and I returned to Watertown, New York for the WPBS-TV art action. It was

Boldt Castle

quite an experience. I was just a little nervous to say the least, to be on the air live for interviews, I did get used to it after the first day. The auction ran for four days and we had a wonderful time.

We also had the opportunity to meet several other artists in the area. The other featured artist Andrew Hoag from Ontario, Canadian artists Gene Canning, Kevin Dodds, Marg Lamendeau, Michael Bellefeuille and American artists Michael Ringer, Dean Richards and Ronald Spooner Sr. to name a few.

Artist Michael Ringer was the host interviewer of the art auction of 2001. Many of Michael's original artwork subjects are from along or on the St. Lawrence River and in the Adirondack Mountains with many commissioned projects from the area. It was great meeting with these artists and learning their style and experiences in the art world.

The exposure of my artwork to this area was wonderful and the people of Northern New York and Southeastern Ontario welcomed me with open arms. The auction opened the doors for a few commissioned projects and my becoming a member the Northern New York Arts Association. I was invited by Lynn Newman, the association chair, to be a guest artist at the association gallery for a weekend in May of 2002 in Sackets Harbor, New York.

In May of 2002, artist Michael Ringer from Alexandria Bay, New York, had taken me on a boat ride on the St. Lawrence River so I could do photography work of Sunken Rock Lighthouse and Boldt Castle along with many other picturesque islands and scenes of the river. As I was doing some photography work on Sunken Rock, a Canadian ore ship was making its way down the river. I was familiar with seeing these large vessels on spacious Lake Superior.

But to see the vessels in the river was awesome. They look so much bigger because of it being on the river, not as spacious as a Great Lake.

There are over 1,700 islands on the St. Lawrence River from Cape Vincent, New York fifty miles to Ogdensburg, New York. It was interesting to see the different islands. Some of the families who owned them, such as the Kelloggs, McNally, Catapillar and the history behind the islands was very revealing. As you travel by boat past some of the islands, you can see the crumpled foundations that used to hold up 400-room grand hotels that were destroyed by fire. Being on an island made it difficult to put the fires out.

Commissioned Projects ...

In July of 2000 we were on a trip to Bayfield, Wisconsin and had stopped at an information office of tourism in Wisconsin and picked up brochures of the area. One of the booklets we picked up was at the Wisconsin Bed & Breakfast Association.

This publication included the Bed & Breakfasts of Wisconsin, the locations of the businesses and photos of the structures. The structures were of various sizes and styles from Country Inns to Queen Victorians. Once again, the subject matter of inns and bed & breakfasts lend themselves well for my style of artwork. Also we are speaking of original and restored structures of the past. People have wonderful memories of growing up or spending time at these structures.

After that trip to Bayfield in July 2000, I kept that publication and the thoughts I had until later that year. At the time, I was still working on lighthouse artwork from the east coast.

In September of 2000, I was guest artist at The Keeper of the Light store in Bayfield. The Keeper of the Light is a store that sells lighthouse and nautical merchandise. Before we left for Bayfield, I looked at the Bed and Breakfasts of Wisconsin booklet I picked up a few months earlier to see what inns were located in Bayfield. They had many beautiful inns listed in the area, one in particular had caught my eye, The Old Rittenhouse Inn.

In past years on our trips to Bayfield, one could not miss this magnificent structure on the hill located on Rittenhouse Avenue. The Victorian Queen style building with its wrap-a-round porch and it's beautiful gardens made it an ideal composition to create a piece of artwork.

Thursday, the day before I was to be guest artist at the Keeper of the Light, I decided to stop by the Old Rittenhouse Inn to see if I could meet the owner, Jerry Phillips. It was around 10:00 a.m. as I entered the Inn and was greeted by an associate of the Inn. I asked if Jerry was in and the associate said he was out but would be returning around 3:00 p.m. I left a few samples of my artwork and a brochure about myself and asked if they would give them to him and I would be returning later in the day.

Later that afternoon I returned to the Inn to see Jerry Phillips. The associate said Jerry wanted to see me. I followed the associate down a hallway and I said it wasn't necessary to interrupt his meeting, but the associate said Jerry wanted to know when I was there. As the associate knocked on the door and opened it slowly, she interrupted his meeting and told him I was here. I was standing in the hallway and I heard Jerry tell the associate, "Set Mr. Peter-

Old Rittenhouse Inn - Bayfield, Wisconsin

son up with a glass of our finest wine, I will meet him on the porch in 10 minutes." As I walked on the wrap-around-porch one could not notice the beautiful hanging baskets of flowers and the view from the porch was wonderful.

As Jerry came out on the porch, we introduced ourselves and started visiting about why I was there. Jerry spoke of the samples artwork how unique and very detailed, defined with character. I then spoke of my intentions. As I explained to Jerry, I was starting my venture into historic structures and I thought that drawings of bed and break-fasts would lend themselves well with my style of artwork and the criteria of subject matters.

I then asked him if I could use the Old Rittenhouse Inn as the start of the bed and breakfast inns, resort inns and hotels. With the use of the Old Rittenhouse Inn image as a marketing tool, I told him I would draw it at no charge. Jerry was delighted with the arrangement and said yes, as long as I draw his other building the Le Chateau Boutin and I was paid for it. We both agreed to it and decided as long as I was in Bayfield through the weekend that I would do the photography work that weekend.

After we talked about the artwork, Jerry mentioned he belonged to this association of bed and breakfasts, at the time was the president of this association. This association was the "Select Registry - Distinguished Inns of North America." He encouraged me to be a part of their convention in Boston in February 2001. He said I would meet members of the association and it would help promote the marketing of my artwork.

Both the Old Rittenhouse Inn and the Le Chateau Boutin were sitting on a hills and he wanted the drawing from a level prospective. He said he had a cherry picker available

Le Chateau Boutin - Bayfield, Wisconsin

and that Saturday afternoon the inn manager picked me up from the Keeper of the Light store and proceeded to the Old Rittenhouse Inn.

The city of Bayfield was built on the side of a hill, so we parked the truck with the cherry picker kitty corner from the inn to get the proper angle. As I climbed into the basket and as it went higher and higher, I was getting a little nervous thinking the truck was going to tip over, Larry assured me everything was OK. I was level with the roof line of the porch, snapped a bunch of photos at different exposures and zoomed into areas of the structure that was difficult to catch with the naked eye. A short time later we headed to the Le Chateau Boutin to do the photo shoot.

It was now later in the afternoon and with all the traffic going by, horns honking from a wedding party, it was quite uncomfortable being in that cherry picker 40 feet above the ground. As I got level with the Le Chateau Boutin, snapped pictures for the reference of my artwork. Through the view finder I noticed a bride was coming out of a door way onto the porch. All of sudden she saw me and was waving to the rest of the wedding party to come onto the porch. They all started posing as though I was their photographer. After a short time, Larry lowered me down to the street and brought me back to the Keeper of the Light store.

A few months later, I completed the drawings of the Old Rittenhouse Inn and the Le Chateau Boutin and Jerry was very happy with the artwork. From the original artwork, we printed note cards and prints and made them available for guests to purchase. Also, the bride found out who I was and what I was doing there on the day of their wedding reception. She had called me to see if I had some pictures of them. I did send them some photos of that day with a print of the Le Chateau Boutin artwork.

In December of 2000, I took a trip to Marshall, Michigan to meet with Susan Moore, the executive director of the Select Registry, to find out a little more information about their association. I had a chance to meet the staff and learn more about the association. I was so impressed I also became an associated member. The Select Registry has over 400 members.

While I was in Michigan, I stayed overnight at The English Inn in Eaton Rapids, Michigan and the next morning I took advantage of the fog and ice crystals on the trees for a perfect photo opportunity. Later in the morning I dropped off artwork information to the National House Inn in Marshall, and traveled to Union City, Michigan to see The Vic-

Office of The Select Registry - Marshall, Michigan

torian Villa Inn.

Owner Ronald Gibson was not at the Inn the day of my visit, but dropped off information about my artwork and myself and decided to take photos of his establishment for future reference.

When I returned to Minnesota, I called Ronald Gibson and explained who I was, that I stopped by The Victorian Villa Inn and asked if he had seen the artwork samples I dropped off at the Inn. He said he had and was impressed with the style and detail. Soon thereafter, Ronald had commissioned me to draw The Victorian Villa Inn.

The Victorian Villa Inn was originally the residence of Dr. and Mrs. William P. and Caroline E. Hurd. Completed in 1876 for the princely sum of $12,000, this incredible building was originally designed and built as a one-family retirement residence for the Hurds. The home has had several owners over the next decades: the Williards from 1910-1930; the Danleys from 1930-1942: the Davis from 1942-1950; and the Cox family from 1950-1978.

The Gibsons purchased the home in 1978 and immediately set about the complete and correct restoration of the by-now dilapidated mansion. In 1978 the once brilliant mansion had become a low-income apartment house with seven different units including sleeping rooms, apartments, a music lesson studio, and a chiropractors office.

The Villa has now been completely restored to its original glory and retrofitted with 10 authentically detailed bedchambers and suites; seven in the main house and three in the carriage house. Opening in January 1982, The Victorian Villa was only the third bed and breakfast inn in Michigan and the sixth Inn in the Midwest.

In February 2001 Kathy and I attended the Select Reg-

The Victorian Villa Inn - Union City, Michigan

istry Conference in Boston, Massachusetts. As a vendor I had meet several owners in the Bed & Breakfast, Hotel and Resort industry. During the conference I was working on The Victorian Villa Inn drawing which allowed the Select Registry members to see the process of how I create my artwork and how I capture the detail.

The conference was also an education for me. Owning an inn is very demanding of one's time but can be very rewarding and satisfying. The conference for me was a very positive experience and resulted in some commissioned projects.

A month later, I found out about another bed & breakfast and innkeepers association the "Professional Association of Innkeepers International" and became an associate member of their organization. Over 4000 members belong to this association and a few months later after I joined, Jerry Phillips (owner of the Rittenhouse Inn in Bayfield, Wisconsin) became executive director of the association.

In May of 2001, I finished a commissioned drawing of the White Lace Inn, located in Sturgeon Bay, Wisconsin. We met Dennis Statz at the Select Registry conference earlier in the year and he commissioned me to draw his inn. Kathy and I delivered the original artwork and stayed at the inn for a few days and enjoyed the beauty of the inn and gardens, as well as taking in some of the sites of Door County.

Dennis and Bonnie Statz had the idea of owning a bed and breakfast and becoming innkeepers after visiting an old mansion in Kentucky in the early 1980s. At that time, Dennis was a mechanical engineer in Indianapolis and Bonnie was a jewelry designer and a batik artist. They were looking for a business opportunity in the New England states and Michigan. In 1982, they continued their search

White Lace Inn - Sturgeon Bay, Wisconsin

and with the suggestion of friends, they returned to their home state of Wisconsin.

They looked for a home in Door County to turn into a bed and breakfast business. They found a dilapidated Queen Anne Victorian home in Sturgeon Bay. When they found this structure, they new this is what they were looking for.

On July 1, 1982, the White Lace Inn opened its doors to its first guests. This is the Main House which has five rooms. The property took on three more structures which became part of the White Lace Inn. In 1983, Dennis and Bonnie purchased an 1880s house that was about to be torn down, moved it onto their property renovated it, and it became the Garden House. The Washburn House was added in 1986 and the Hadley House was finished in 1996, bringing the total number of rooms to the property to 18. Many weddings have taken place in the gazebo surrounded by beautiful gardens and ponds.

Chuck Flanders, general manager of the Castle Hill Inn, commissioned me to draw the mansion portion of the resort in May of 2001. This was a very unique setting with a lighthouse near the property. I actually visited that particular lighthouse "Castle Hill" in February 2000. I did notice the Castle Hill Inn, but I had no idea that it was an inn. It is located in the city of Newport, Rhode Island.

Creating this piece of artwork was very challenging with all the detail in the building, the landscape and the lighthouse. It took nearly 60 hours to complete. The results were very satisfying.

Castle Hill was built in 1874 as a summer home for Harvard marine biologist Alexander Agassiz. Today, the Castle

Castle Hill Inn & Resort - Newport, Rhode Island

Hill Inn retains the warmth and quiet luxury of the 19th century seacoast life. The Castle Hill Inn is made up of four structures on the property, the Agassiz Mansion (The Inn), Harbor House Rooms, Beach House Rooms and the Chalet.

The Castle Hill Lighthouse sits just south of the inn. This 34-foot lighthouse is nestled in the hill surrounded by various rock formations overlooking the water between the Atlantic Ocean and Narragansett Bay.

The Garth Woodside Mansion, a Second Empire Victorian mansion is a beautiful bed and breakfast inn located in Hannibal, Missouri. In the early 1870s, the Garth family purchased a farm just outside Hannibal and built a large summer home, which they named "Woodside."On occasion, the Garth family entertained and corresponded with childhood friend Samuel Clemens (Mark Twain).

The mansion was a family home until the 1970s. Tours of the mansion were open to the public until the late 1980's when it was turned into a bed and breakfast business. Present owners John and Julie Rolsen purchased the property in 1999. The entire first floor has been restored, not renovated back to its 1870's splendor. I was commissioned to draw the Garth Woodside Mansion by John and Julie in June of 2001.

It is a real education when you discover the history of these homes and mansions. It is wonderful to meet the owners, to hear about their restoration projects, see the woodwork, stairways, antiques, tiffany windows, fireplaces, porches, all the things that add charm and character as well as the grounds, gardens and ponds. I feel very fortunate to capture the detail and charm of these images through the view finder of my camera and to be able to create a portrait of these beautiful structures in the style of

Garth Woodside Mansion - Hannibal, Missouri

pointillism.

Over the next several months I created more original pieces of artwork to add to my collection and a few commissioned projects. I also did illustrations for a childrens book "Fiat Lux" which means Let there be light! written by Dave Strzok from Bayfield, Wisconsin.

During a guest artist appearance in Sackets Harbors, New York in June 2002, I received a phone call from Carmen Drake of Chattanooga, Tennessee. She was inquiring about my services of commissioned artwork. She had received a information packet about my artwork at the April 2002 Professional Association of Innkeepers International Convention in Chicago, Illinois.

Carmen and her husband Gene purchased the Mayor's Mansion Inn and were looking to have a portrait of the inn. After discussing the project and sending proposal, Gene and Carmen want to proceed with commissioned project. They had decided to have me come to the Mayor's Mansion Inn because the proportion and angle were important and they were also considering changes to the landscape in the front area of the mansion.

The weekend after I returned from New York, I finished my work week at ECM Publishers, Inc., on Saturday I flew to Atlanta, picked up a rental car and drove to Chattanooga, Tennessee. I arrived at the Mayor's Mansion Inn around 2:00 p.m. and settled in to my room. After resting for about an hour I returned to the main entryway and met Gene and Carmen Drake.

We went outside to look at the mansion, looked at different angles and discussed the landscape changes. I then proceeded to do a photo shoot for the next few hours. That evening I had dinner with the Drakes and they told me

Mayor's Mansion Inn - Chattanooga, Tennessee

about the history of the inn and some of the interior restoration projects. The next morning with the sun in a different position I snapped a few more rolls of film of the inn and then headed back to Atlanta to catch my flight back to Minneapolis that afternoon.

Among the different styles of homes in the neighborhood (the historic Fort Wood District), the Mayor's Mansion Inn, built in 1889, is the only house clearly Victorian Romanesque. The stone surface, arches, decorative tiles, and stone trim make this building very distinctive in the district and in the city.

The Whitney Hotel was a commissioned project in 1993. The hotel was restored from a grain elevator and warehouse which sits on the Mississippi River in Minneapolis, Minnesota. Today it is a Hyatt Hotel. The State Capitol of

State Capitol
St.Paul, Minnesota

St. Paul, Minnesota (shown on the previous page) is one of my earlier originals that I added to my collection in 1991.

In November of 2002, my travels took me to the Eastern Seaboard of New Jersey. Future commissioned projects took me to The Duke of Windsor Inn, owned by Patricia Joyce in Cape May and the Victorian House, a bed and breakfast owned by Lynne and Alan Kaplan in Spring Lake.

While I was out east, I also had the opportunity to take photos of lighthouses for future references, Barnegat Light, Twin Lights of Navesink, Sandy Hook, Cape May and Sea Girt.

As I complete this book I could not forget the city where Kathy and I have spent the past 20 years, Forest Lake, Minnesota. The city our children grew up in, the celebrations, the friendships, the businesses, service organizations and the wonderful memories we will never forget. Just like many other cities in this country, Forest Lake is going through many changes. Many of the old buildings are being torn down to make way for new business.

The artwork of Za Pizzeria was a commissioned project by Paul Deuth of Forest Lake. This building has much history behind it in the city of Forest Lake. In the 1930s the structure was part of an oil station business.

The artwork of the "Forest Lake, Minnesota 1990" shows the beach and park area, as well as the water tower which in my mind and in the minds of many people in the area, remains one of the last real icons of Forest Lake. This was before the Wal Marts, Targets, Menards and so on. Today, we become so much closer to being a suburb of a big city. This is change and this is reality, but don't forget the past.

'Za Pizzeria in Forest Lake, Minnesota

Forest Lake, Minnesota 1990

Many thanks to the volunteers at the parks and lighthouses. The stories and information that I received was appreciated and a big part of my adventures.

Many thanks to the information received from the bed and breakfast inns and resort owners.

Referenced material used with permission from the 3rd edition of "Seaway Trail Lighthouses"
Seaway Trail, Inc.
Corner of W. Main & Ray Streets
Sackets Harbor, NY 13685
www.seawaytrail.com

Index of Artwork

Index of Artwork

Index of Artwork

*Photographs by Randall J. Peterson

All artwork created by Randall J. Peterson. Dates in parenthesis indicate when the year the artwork was completed.

Epilogue

The idea for this book came to me after an accident in which I rolled my car on icy roads the morning of December 10, 2001. I was very fortunate to walk away from it with no injuries. Being a cat lover and a owner of two cats, I feel they gave me one of their nine lives.

I have done many original pieces of artwork and many thousands of limited edition prints. Shortly after the accident, I realized I needed to share my adventures, why I choose my subjects and the thoughts behind my artwork.

My artwork and the marketing of it could not have been possible without the help and support of my family, friends, collectors, the people who have commissioned me to do originals and the people who have purchased prints over the years.

If I were to leave a legacy, I would hope that through my artwork, I will touch the hearts of all ages from the young to the elderly. By reading about my artwork and by visualizing it, I hope to encourage people of all ages to use their talents to create original artwork.

In the end, I hope to bring an awareness of the many historic landmarks we have. It is a desire to preserve these sites and buildings by loving and thoughtful restoration.